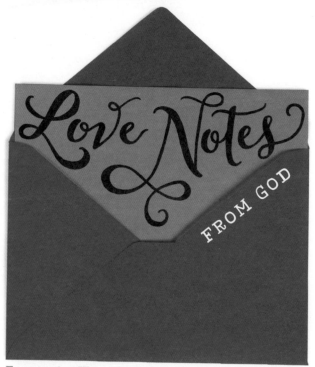

Encouraging Words from the One who Loves You Most

AS IMAGINED BY
JAY PAYLEITNER

We love because he first loved us.

I JOHN 4:19 NIV

Imagine receiving a personal love note from God.

Does that sound impossible? If you stay mindful, you'll realize He is constantly sending you messages of encouragement, comfort, guidance, and inspiration.

He wants you to know and feel His love.

He wants you to experience the joy of a full life and the exhilaration of digging deep and doing great things. He invites you to follow, trust, and rest in him.

God delivers messages of love 24/7/365. In nature by way of raindrops, thunderbolts, and sunsets. Through friends, family, neighbors, and strangers. In words you hear, read, write, dream, and imagine.

The love notes in this little book were inspired by God's Word. Delivered to you at exactly the right time. Because He knows exactly what you need.

Just to confirm: God invented love. God is love. His greatest gift is the ability we have to give and receive love.

The fact that God loves you is the truest thing about you.

Got the message?

Do to others
what you would
have them do to you.

MATTHEW 7:12 NIV

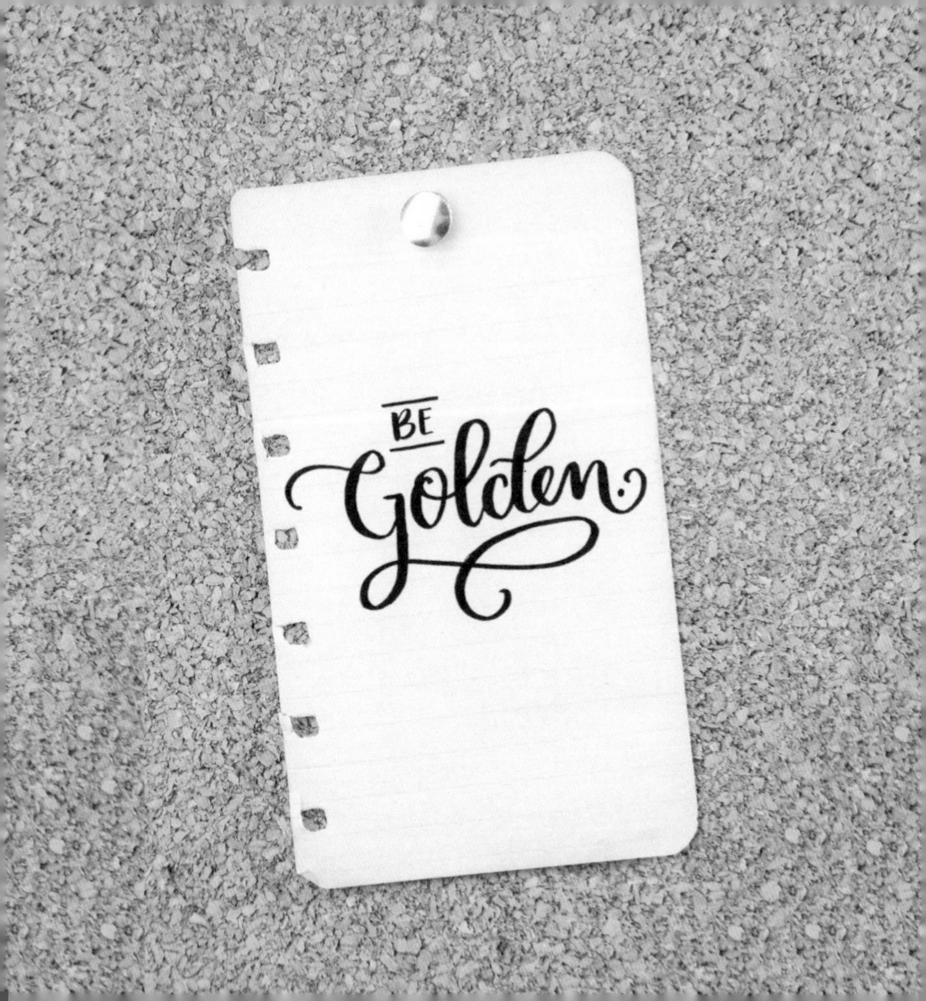
BE
Golden.

For the word of God is alive
and powerful. It is sharper than
the sharpest two-edged sword,
cutting between soul and spirit,
between joint and marrow.
It exposes our innermost
thoughts and desires.

HEBREWS 4:12 NLT

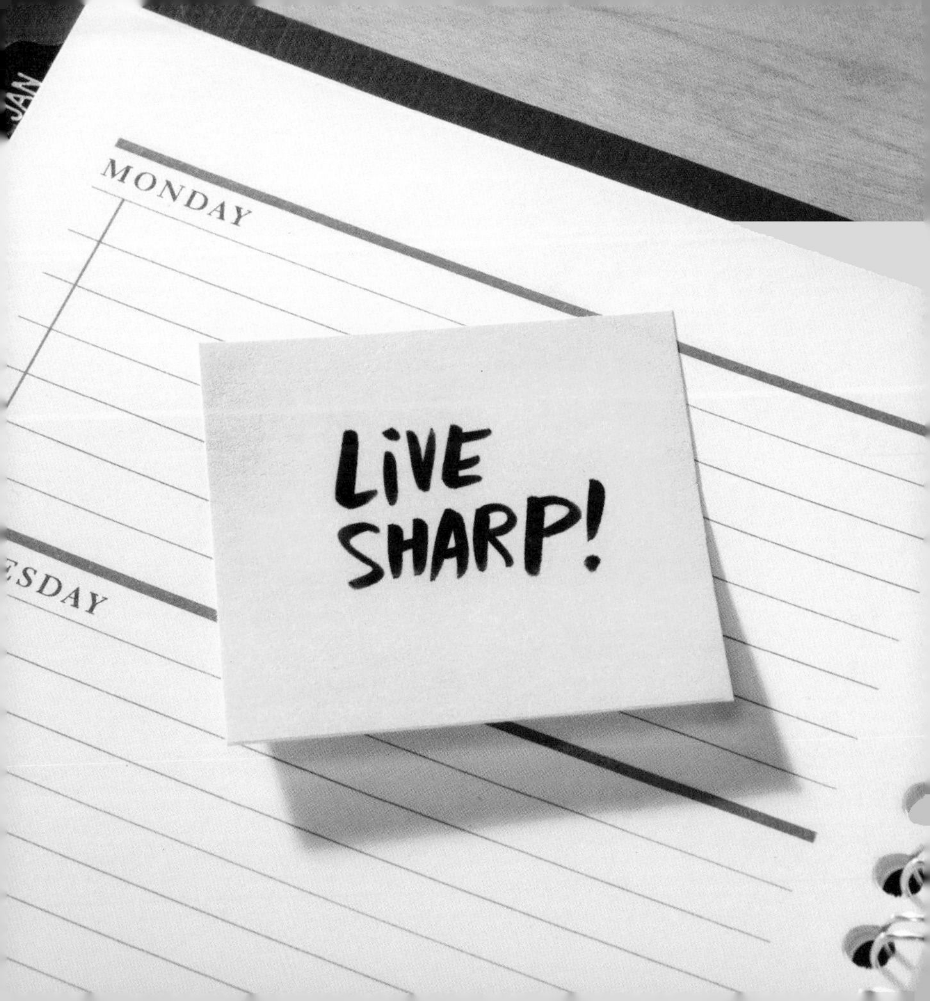
JAN
MONDAY
LIVE SHARP!

He lifted me out of the slimy pit,
out of the mud and mire;
He set my feet on a rock and
gave me a firm place to stand.

PSALM 40:2 NIV

Do not fear, for I am with you;
Do not anxiously look
about you, for I am your God.
I will strengthen you,
surely I will help you,
Surely I will uphold you
with My righteous right hand.

ISAIAH 41:10 NASB

What you think
you can't do...
I can help
you do.

Anyone who belongs to Christ
has become a new person.
The old life is gone;
a new life has begun!

II CORINTHIANS 5:17 NLT

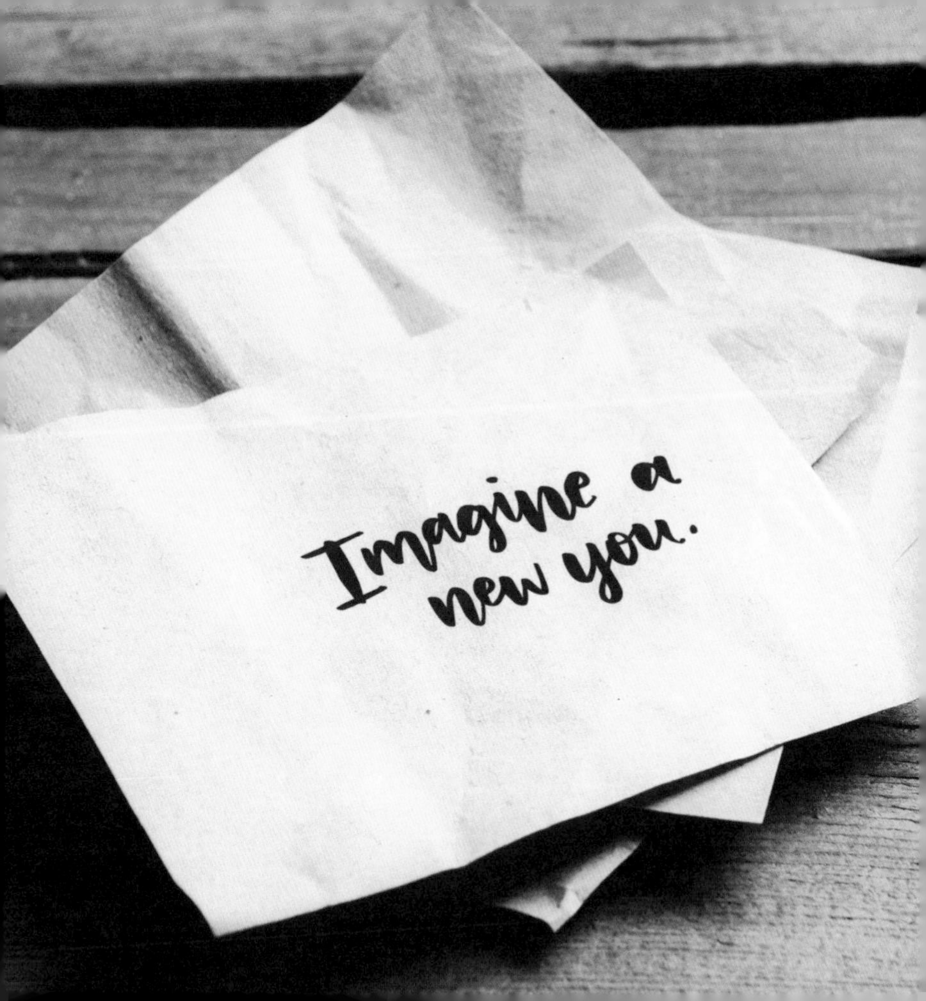
Imagine a
new you.

My cup overflows
with blessings.
Surely Your goodness
and unfailing love
will pursue me
all the days of my life.

PSALM 23:5,6 NLT

Don't cry
over spilt
anything.

Now is your time of grief,
but I will see you again
and you will rejoice, and no one
will take away your joy.

JOHN 16:22 NIV

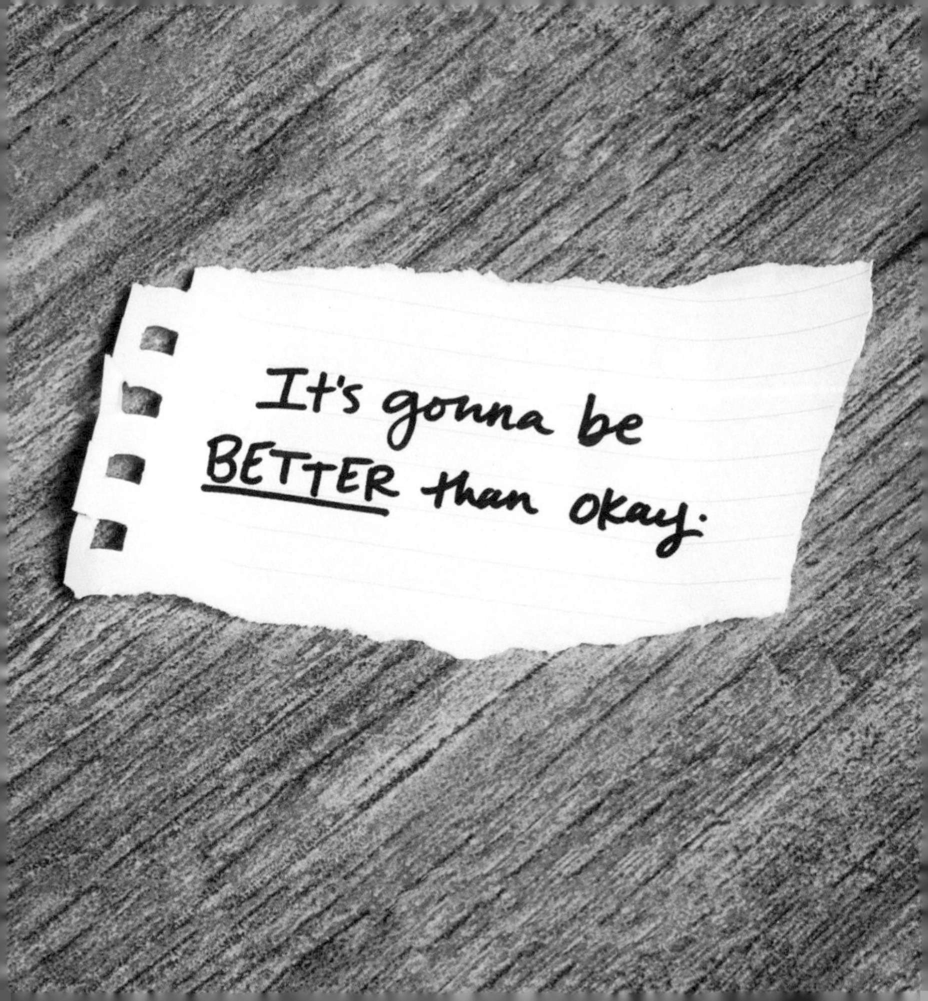
It's gonna be
BETTER than okay.

Come to Me,
all you who are weary
and burdened,
and I will give you rest.

MATTHEW 11:28 NIV

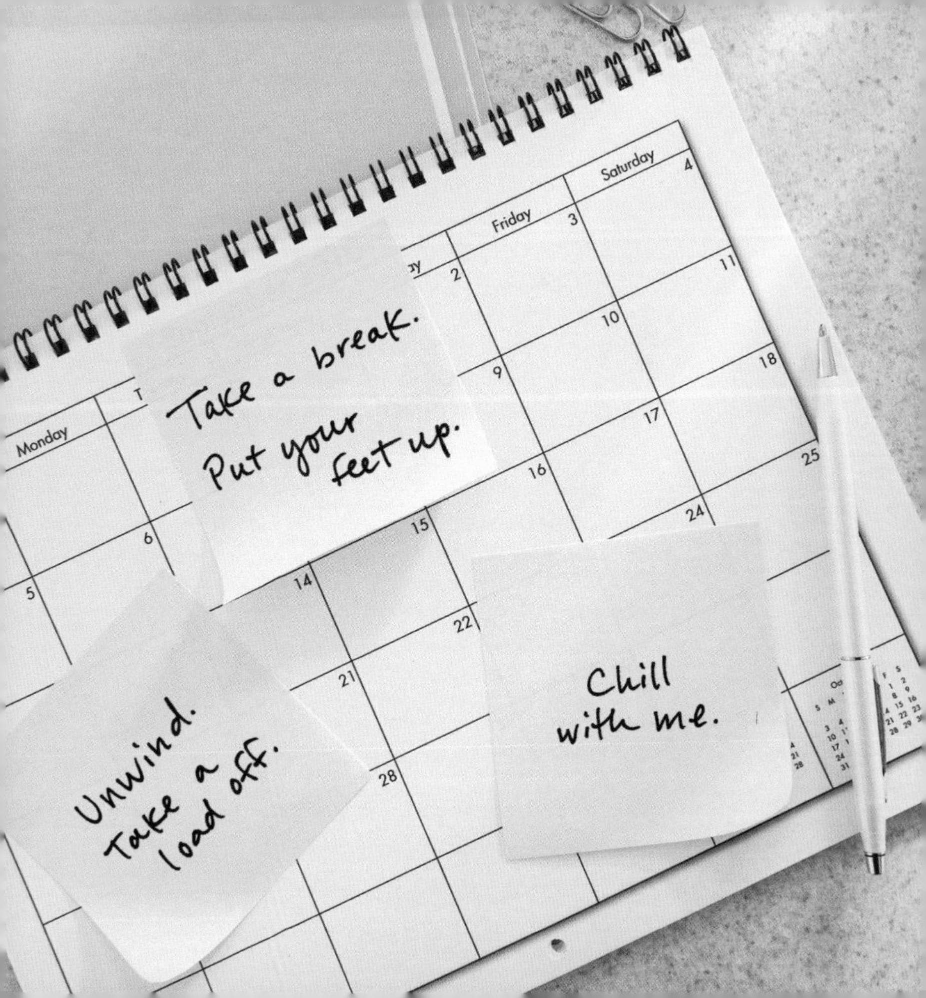
Take a break.
Put your feet up.
Unwind.
Take a load off.
Chill with me.
Monday
Friday
Saturday

So don't worry about tomorrow, for tomorrow will bring its own worries. Today's trouble is enough for today.

MATTHEW 6:34 NLT

Do not let your hearts
be troubled.
You believe in God;
believe also in Me.

JOHN 14:1 NIV

POST CARD

CARTE POSTALE

JUST

believe.

Forget the former things;
do not dwell on the past.
See, I am doing a new thing!
Now it springs up; do you not
perceive it? I am making a way
in the wilderness
and streams in the wasteland.

ISAIAH 43:18-19 NIV

Say ADIOS to
yesterday.
I've got
Something new
just for you.

Everything is possible
for one who believes.

MARK 9:23 NIV

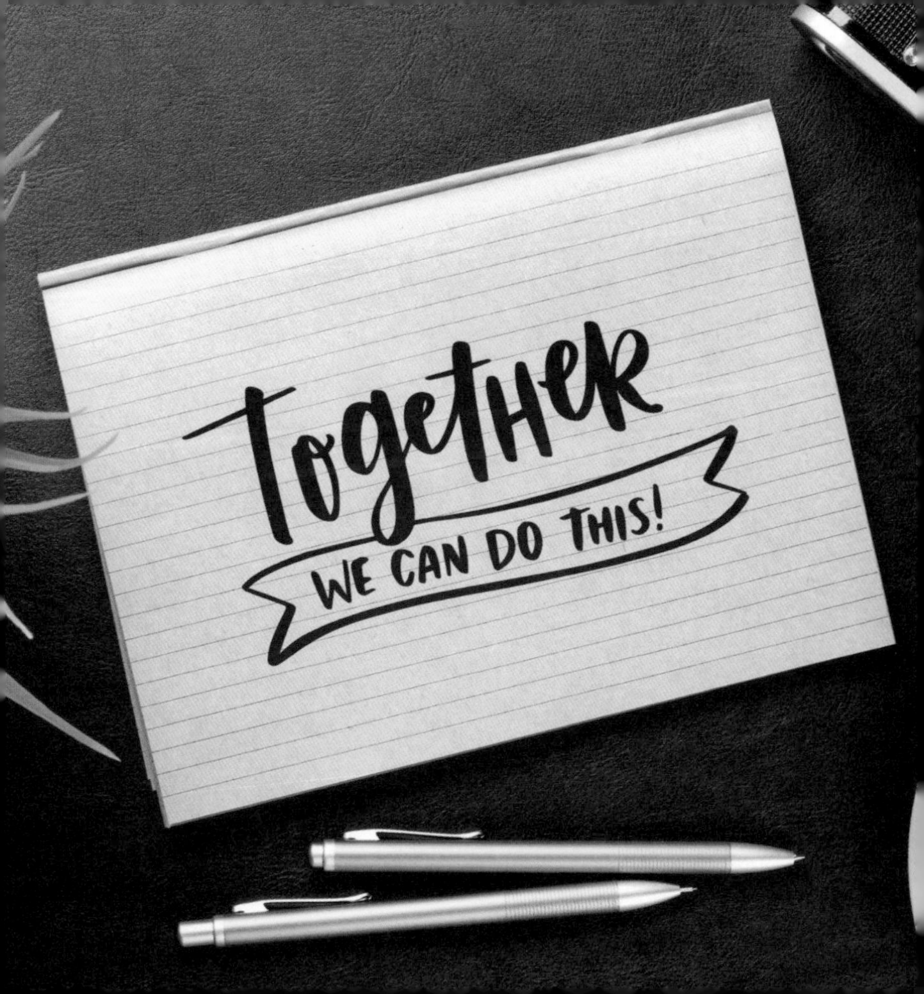
Together
WE CAN DO THIS!

Whether you turn
to the right or to the left,
your ears will hear a voice
behind you, saying,
"This is the way; walk in it."

ISAIAH 30:21 NIV

You are all children of the
light and children of the day.
We do not belong to the night
or to the darkness.

I THESSALONIANS 5:5 NIV

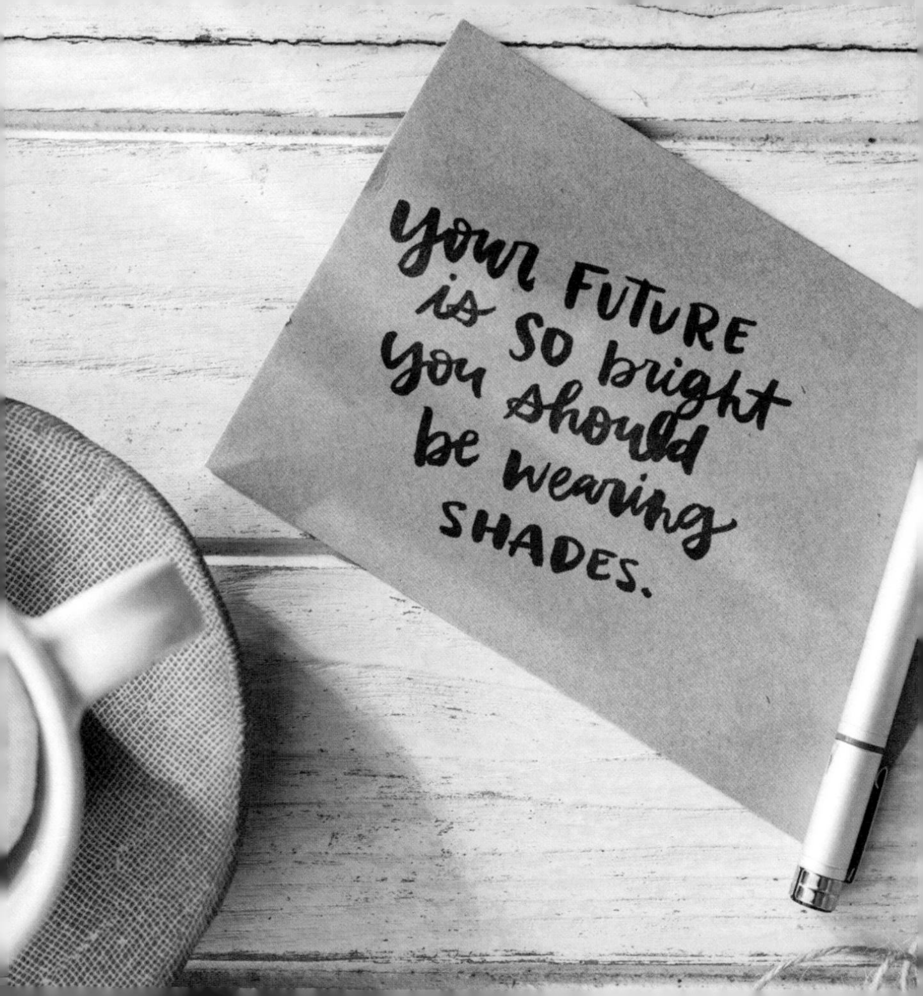
your FUTURE
is SO bright
you should
be wearing
SHADES.

When I see the rainbow
in the clouds, I will remember
the eternal covenant
between God and every
living creature on earth.

GENESIS 9:16 NLT

Be still, and know
that I am God.

PSALM 46:10 NIV

Stop.
Think.
Believe.

Know me,
so you can
know yourself.

But God demonstrates
His own love for us in this:
While we were still sinners,
Christ died for us.

ROMANS 5:8 NIV

For it is God who works in you
to will and to act in order to
fulfill His good purpose.

PHILIPPIANS 2:13 NIV

I've got
a plan.

And you're
part of it.

For everything there is a season,
a time for every activity under heaven.
A time to be born and a time to die.
A time to plant and a time to harvest.
A time to kill and a time to heal.
A time to tear down and a time to build up.
A time to cry and a time to laugh.
A time to grieve and a time to dance.
A time to scatter stones
and a time to gather stones.
A time to embrace and a time to turn away.
A time to search and a time to quit searching.
A time to keep and a time to throw away.
A time to tear and a time to mend.
A time to be quiet and a time to speak.
A time to love and a time to hate.
A time for war and a time for peace.

ECCLESIASTES 3:1-8 NLT

Yet what we suffer now is nothing compared to the glory He will reveal to us later.

ROMANS 8:18 NLT

It may be difficult to believe right now, but there's joy just around the corner.

$\longrightarrow$

All Scripture is God-breathed
and is useful for teaching,
rebuking, correcting and
training in righteousness.

II TIMOTHY 3:16 NIV

my

WORD

works.

He is so rich in kindness and grace that He purchased our freedom with the blood of His Son and forgave our sins.

EPHESIANS 1:7 NLT

OPEN TIME:
DATE :

Bill Check

SUBTOTAL
TOTAL

AT

I'm buying!

** Thank you Please come again **

Submit yourselves, then,
to God. Resist the devil,
and he will flee from you.
Come near to God,
and He will come near to you.

JAMES 4:7-8 NIV

I've
got your
back.

Put on the full armor of God,
so that you can take your stand
against the devil's schemes.

EPHESIANS 6:11 NIV

Carry each other's burdens,
and in this way you will fulfill
the law of Christ.

GALATIANS 6:2 NIV

MONDAY

SDAY

Whose load
can you
lighten today?

The Lord Himself goes before
you and will be with you;
He will never leave you nor
forsake you. Do not be afraid;
do not be discouraged.

DEUTERONOMY 31:8 NIV

It's simple really.
Just. Follow. Me.

I can do all things
through Him
who strengthens me.

PHILIPPIANS 4:13 NASB

For our light and momentary
troubles are achieving for us
an eternal glory that far
outweighs them all.

II CORINTHIANS 4:17 NIV

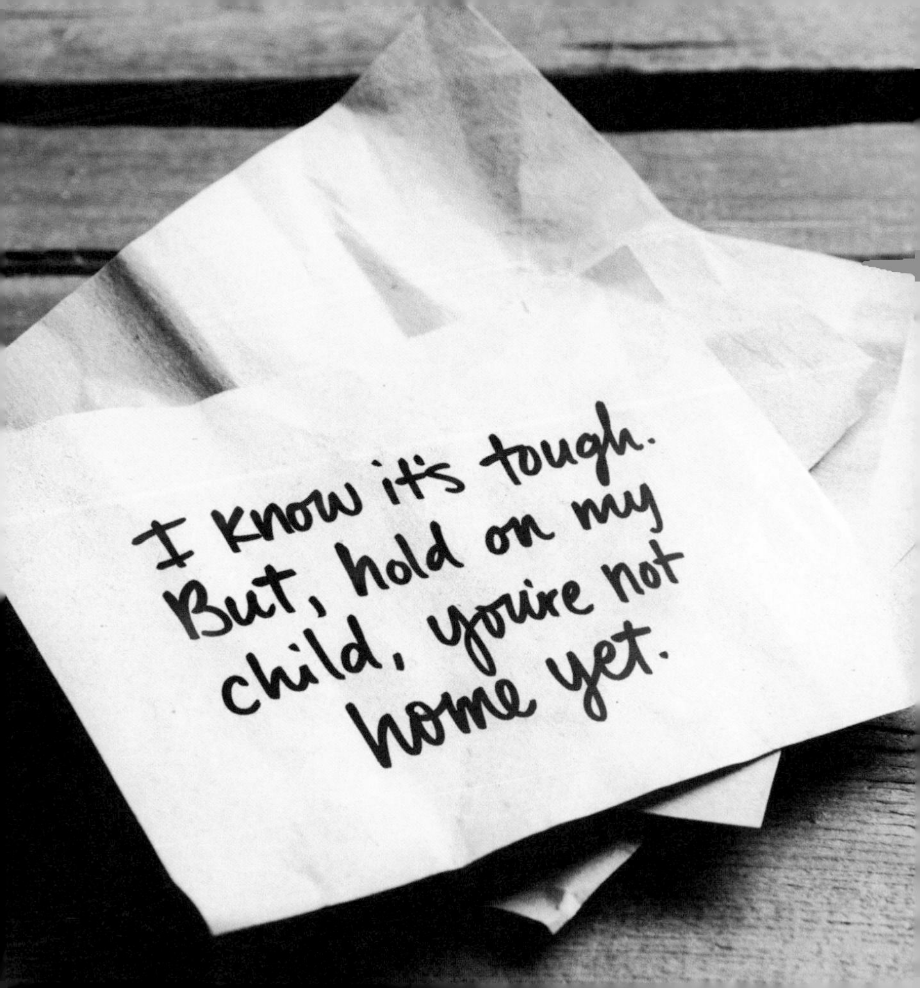
I know it's tough.
But, hold on my
child, you're not
home yet.

For every child of God defeats
this evil world, and we achieve
this victory through our faith.

I JOHN 5:4 NLT

Watch and pray so that you
will not fall into temptation.
The spirit is willing,
but the flesh is weak.

MATTHEW 26:41 NIV

Therefore encourage one another and build each other up, just as in fact you are doing.

I THESSALONIANS 5:11 NIV

Monday
Friday
Saturday
You have the power to make someone's DAY.

No temptation has overtaken you except what is common to mankind. And God is faithful; He will not let you be tempted beyond what you can bear. But when you are tempted, He will also provide a way out so that you can endure it.

I CORINTHIANS 10:13 NIV

Nothing is
going to
happen
today we
can't handle
together.

Trust in the Lord
with all your heart
and lean not on your own
understanding.

PROVERBS 3:5 NIV

POST CARD

CARTE POSTALE

trust me.

I press on toward the goal
to win the prize for which
God has called me heavenward
in Christ Jesus.

PHILIPPIANS 3:14 NIV

Don't be afraid, little flock.
For it gives your Father
great happiness to give you
the Kingdom.

LUKE 12:32 NLT

I'm delighted
to say everything
I have is yours.

You make known to me
the path of life;
in your presence there is
fullness of joy;
at your right hand
are pleasures forevermore.

PSALM 16:11 ESV

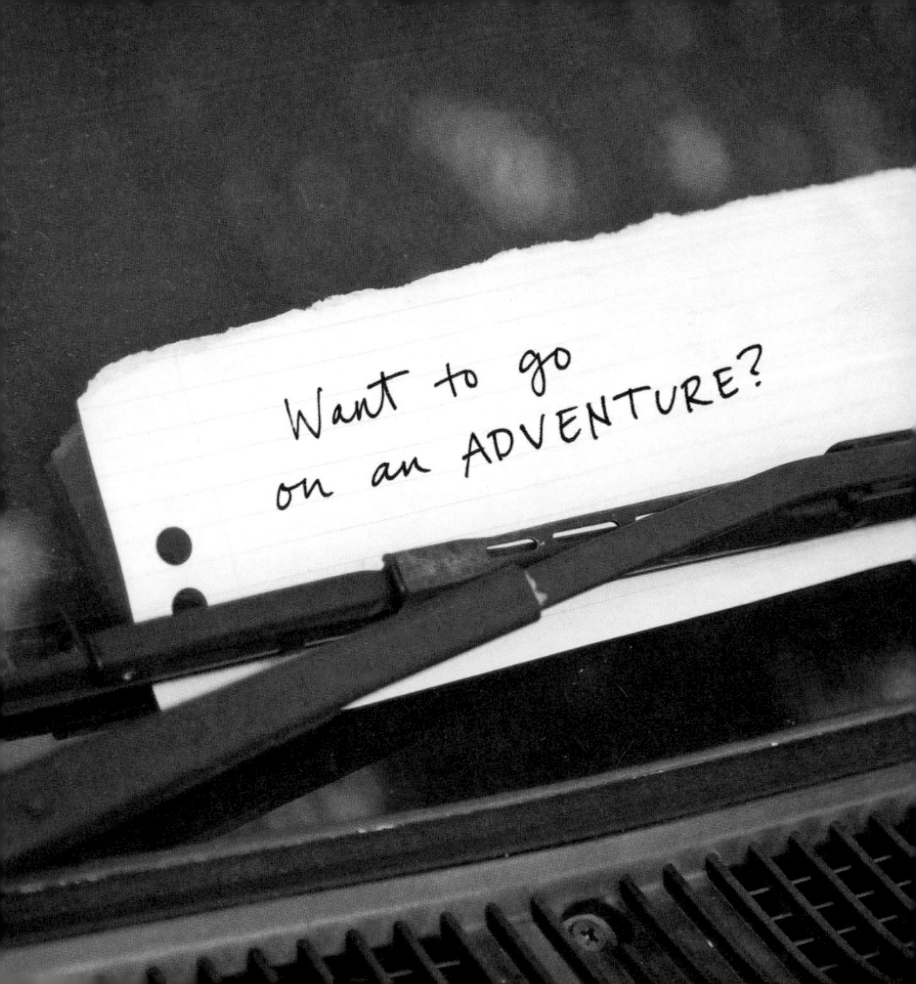
Want to go
on an ADVENTURE?

The thief comes only to steal
and kill and destroy;
I came that they may have life,
and have it abundantly.

JOHN 10:10 NASB

You have
every right
to live
exuberantly.

So he returned home to his father. And while he was still a long way off, his father saw him coming. Filled with love and compassion, he ran to his son, embraced him, and kissed him.

LUKE 15:20 NLT

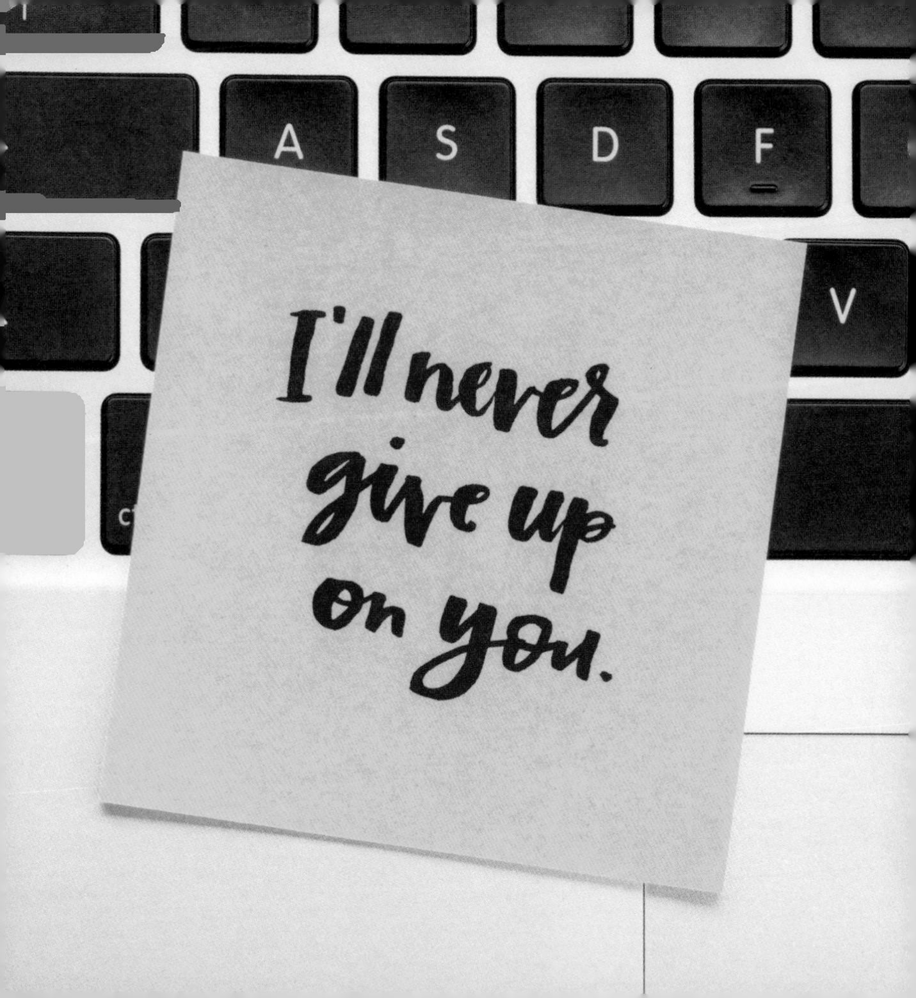
I'll never
give up
on you.
A
S
D
F
V

Surely I am with you always,
to the very end of the age.

MATTHEW 28:20 NIV

If I go and prepare
a place for you,
I will come again
and receive you to Myself,
that where I am,
there you may be also.

JOHN 14:3 NASB

He must increase,
but I must decrease.

JOHN 3:30 NASB

If you try to hang on
to your life, you will lose it.
But if you give up your life
for My sake and for the sake of
the Good News, you will save it.

MARK 8:35 NLT

If you let go,
I promise to
catch you.

Three things will last forever—faith, hope, and love—and the greatest of these is love.

I CORINTHIANS 13:13 NLT

And let us not neglect our meeting together, as some people do, but encourage and warn each other, especially now that the day of His coming back again is drawing near.

HEBREWS 10:25 NLT

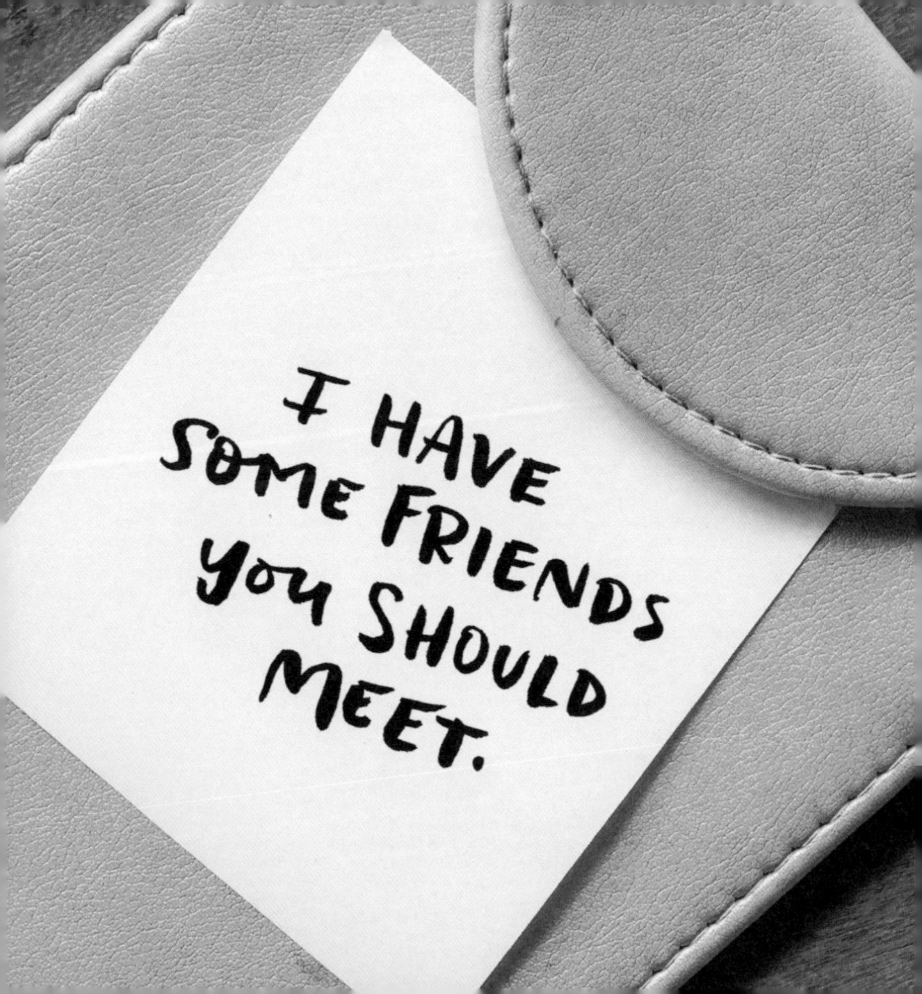
I HAVE
SOME FRIENDS
YOU SHOULD
MEET.

So we fix our eyes not on what
is seen, but on what is unseen,
since what is seen is temporary,
but what is unseen is eternal.

II CORINTHIANS 4:18 NIV

For you know quite well that the day of the Lord will come unexpectedly, like a thief in the night.

I THESSALONIANS 5:2 NLT

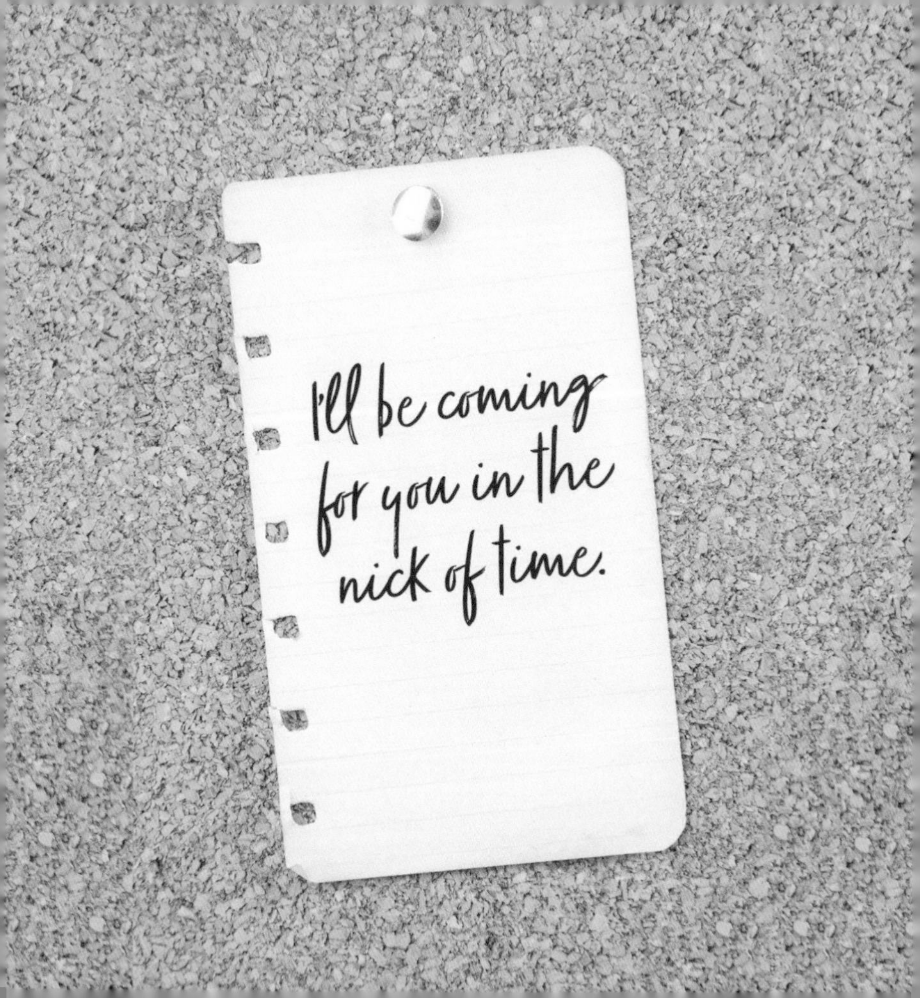
I'll be coming for you in the nick of time.

"For I know the plans
I have for you," declares
the Lord, "plans to prosper you
and not to harm you, plans to
give you hope and a future.

JEREMIAH 29:11 NIV

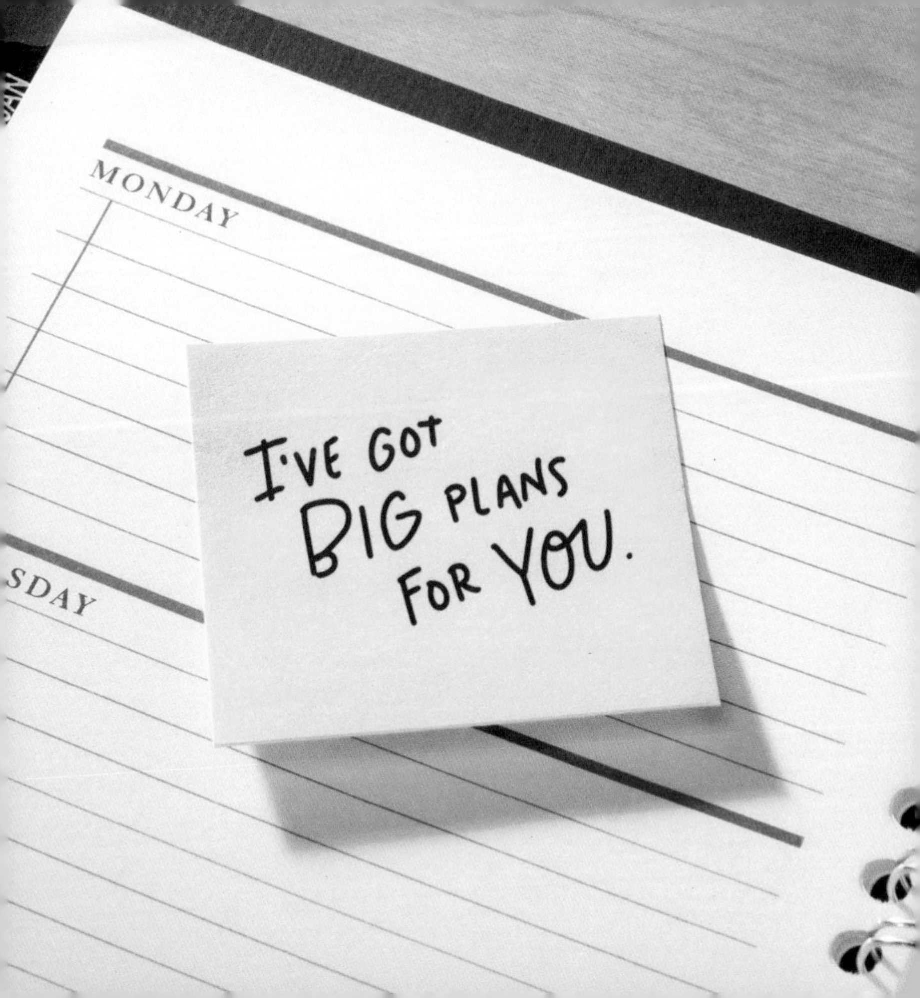
MONDAY
SDAY
I'VE GOT
BIG PLANS
FOR YOU.

For all who are led
by the Spirit of God
are children of God.

ROMANS 8:14 NLT

Imagine being a kid again.

Not that I have already obtained all this, or have already arrived at my goal, but I press on to take hold of that for which Christ Jesus took hold of me. Brothers and sisters, I do not consider myself yet to have taken hold of it. But one thing I do: Forgetting what is behind and straining toward what is ahead, I press on toward the goal to win the prize for which God has called me heavenward in Christ Jesus.

PHILIPPIANS 3:12-14

We know that God causes
everything to work together
for the good of those who love
God and are called according to
His purpose for them.

ROMANS 8:28 NLT

If you're on my team,
all that stuff you're worrying about...
it's going to work out just fine.

Repay no one evil for evil,
but give thought to do what is
honorable in the sight of all.
If possible, so far as it depends
on you, live peaceably with all.
Beloved, never avenge
yourselves, but leave it to the
wrath of God, for it is written,
"Vengeance is mine,
I will repay, says the Lord."

ROMANS 12:17-19 ESV

Don't let the KNUCKLEHEADS get you down.

Honor your father and your mother, so that you may live long in the land the Lord your God is giving you.

EXODUS 20:12 NIV

When the disciples saw Him walking on the sea, they were terrified, and said, "It is a ghost!" And they cried out in fear. But immediately Jesus spoke to them, saying, "Take courage, it is I; do not be afraid." Peter said to Him, "Lord, if it is You, command me to come to You on the water." And He said, "Come!"

MATTHEW 14:26-29 NASB

I think it's
time to step out
of the boat.

Every valley shall be filled in,
every mountain and hill
made low. The crooked roads
shall become straight,
the rough ways smooth.

LUKE 3:5 NIV

Winding roads lead to the most beautiful destinations.

For now we see in a mirror
dimly, but then face to face.
Now I know in part;
then I shall know fully,
even as I have been fully known.

I CORINTHIANS 13:12 ESV

You need not
fear what the
future may
hold because
I hold the
future.

I will never leave you
nor forsake you.

JOSHUA 1:5 NIV

Those who hope in the Lord
will renew their strength.
They will soar on wings
like eagles; they will run
and not grow weary,
they will walk and not be faint.

ISAIAH 40:31 NIV

For by grace you have been
saved through faith.
And this is not your own doing;
it is the gift of God.

EPHESIANS 2:8 ESV

Do not conform
to the pattern of this world,
but be transformed by
the renewing of your mind.
Then you will be able to test
and approve what God's will is—
His good, pleasing and perfect will.

ROMANS 12:2 NIV

The way of
the world
is not the way
of the wise.

For I am convinced that neither death nor life, neither angels nor demons, neither the present nor the future, nor any powers, neither height nor depth, nor anything else in all creation, will be able to separate us from the love of God that is in Christ Jesus our Lord.

ROMANS 8:38-39 NIV

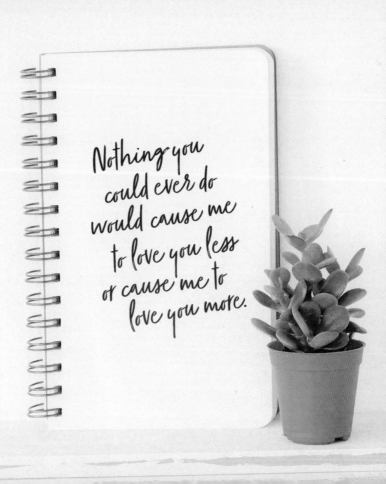

Blessed is the one whose
transgressions are forgiven,
whose sins are covered.
Blessed is the one whose
sin the Lord does not count
against them and in whose
spirit is no deceit.

PSALM 32:1-2 NIV

DaySpring
LIVE YOUR FAITH

Dear Friend,

This book was prayerfully crafted with you, the reader, in mind—every word, every sentence, every page—was thoughtfully written, designed, and packaged to encourage you...right where you are this very moment. At DaySpring, our vision is to see every person experience the life-changing message of God's love. So, as we worked through rough drafts, design changes, edits and details, we prayed for you to deeply experience His unfailing love, indescribable peace, and pure joy. It is our sincere hope that through these Truth-filled pages your heart will be blessed, knowing that God cares about you—your desires and disappointments, your challenges and dreams.

He knows. He cares. He loves you unconditionally.

BLESSINGS!
THE DAYSPRING BOOK TEAM

Additional copies of this book and
other DaySpring titles can be purchased
at fine bookstores everywhere.
Order online at <u>dayspring.com</u>
or
by phone at 1-877-751-4347